NIGHT FLIER

BY ELIZABETH RING
PHOTOGRAPHS BY DWIGHT KUHN

The Millbrook Press
Brookfield, Connecticut

FOR DAVID AND BRIAN

Several of the photographs and portions of the text of
this book appeared in *Ranger Rick,* the National Wildlife Federation magazine for children, in July 1989.

Library of Congress Cataloging-in-Publication Data
Ring, Elizabeth, 1920—
Night flier / by Elizabeth Ring ; photographs by Dwight Kuhn.
p.   cm.
Summary: Lyrical text and exceptional close-up photographs
combine to create a unique presentation of the life cycle
of the cecropia moth. Additional facts about these moths are
presented in a special reference section at the end.

ISBN 1-56294-467-3 (LIB.)   ISBN 1-56294-738-9 (TR.)
1. Cecropia moth—Juvenile literature. [1. Moths.]   I. Kuhn,
Dwight, ill. II.   Title.
QL561.S2R56 1994 595.78′1—dc20 93-40115 CIP AC

Published by The Millbrook Press
2 Old New Milford Road, Brookfield, Connecticut 06804

NIGHT FLIER

Good-bye, moth. I wish you could stay. But night's coming soon. You're a night flier, and you have lots to do. You're almost ready to go. Your new wings are fluttering.

I've watched you all afternoon, since you left your cocoon. You're a brand-new cecropia moth—as big and beautiful as any butterfly I've ever seen. I think I'll name you Half Moon, for the moon shape in the powdery scales of your wings.

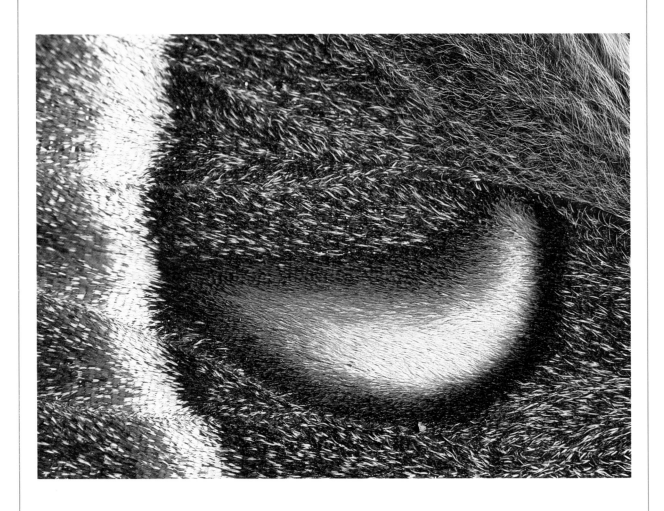

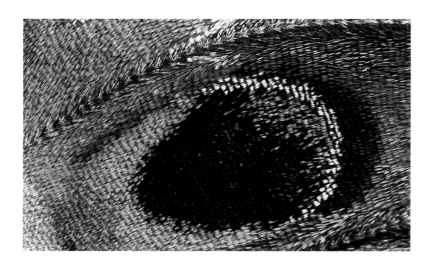

Or maybe I'll call you Teardrop, for that other neat shape I see.

Or perhaps Leopard or Tiger, for the furry-looking spots and stripes on your body.

In a very short while, you will mate. In fact, your mate may be seeking you now. His feathery antennae, waving like plumes over his head, will lead him to your side. Although many male moths may find you, just one will become your mate.

Led by your scent, your mate will sense where you are—no matter how dark the night. Your bodies will meet to make next year's cecropia moths. Then your mate will soon die.

You have more time—a few days to live. You will lay your pearl-like eggs on the leaves of a cherry tree—or perhaps on an apple or a maple, or a lilac or a willow. Then you, too, will die.

After you've gone, your eggs will cling to the leaves for ten days or so.

Then each egg will hatch into a caterpillar. At once, each caterpillar will begin chewing the leaf it just hatched on.

Your offspring will grow as you did—though, of course, you don't remember at all how you grew! As a very young caterpillar you were all bristles. You looked like a small bottle brush, but you were really a leaf-eating machine!

Just as you grew last year, your caterpillar children will get so fat that they will burst right out of their skins. Presto! Like magicians changing disguises, they will shed their bristles and step out in new suits. All summer long they will eat and grow. They will change skins several more times. When they are full grown, each one will look like a shiny green space monster with rose-colored horns.

One fall day, when your caterpillars have stored enough fat to live on through the winter, they will stop eating. Each of your young ones will start to weave its cocoon on a twig or branch of a tree. It will know what to do without being taught. Like a dancer, it will move its head back and forth, back and forth, in slow motion. A fine, strong, silk thread will spin out of the spinneret near its jaws, building the outside of the cocoon first, then the inside walls. The cocoon will be the caterpillar's winter home.

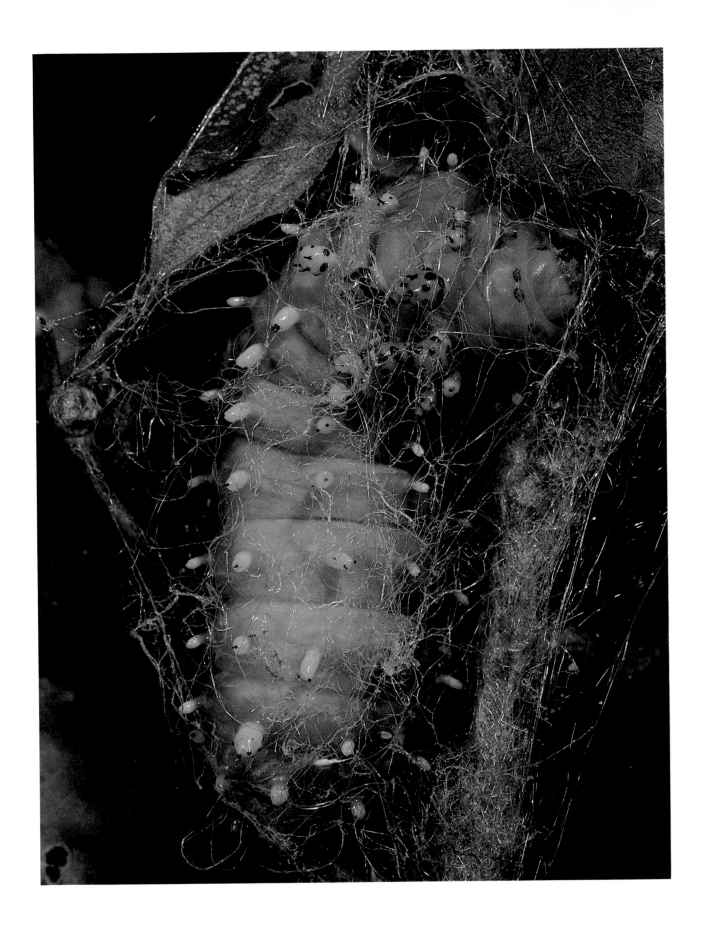

I knew *you* were going to be a cecropia moth
when I found your cocoon one cold day late
last fall. It was a small brown wrinkled bag on
the branch of our cherry tree. Inside, I knew,
you were snug and safe from the rain and cold.
But I brought you home anyway to spend the
winter here on my porch.

I wanted to meet you when you came out this spring. And today, with the sun nice and warm, I watched you come out of the small hole you'd made in your cocoon. First I saw your head, then your legs, then your antennae. Your legs waved like a tiny windmill as you pulled your wet wings through the hole. Then you rested.

At first, your wings—all crumpled together—were no bigger than my thumbnail. Then slowly, slowly, they started to unfold. Your wings grew larger and larger as blood pumped into them, making them swell.

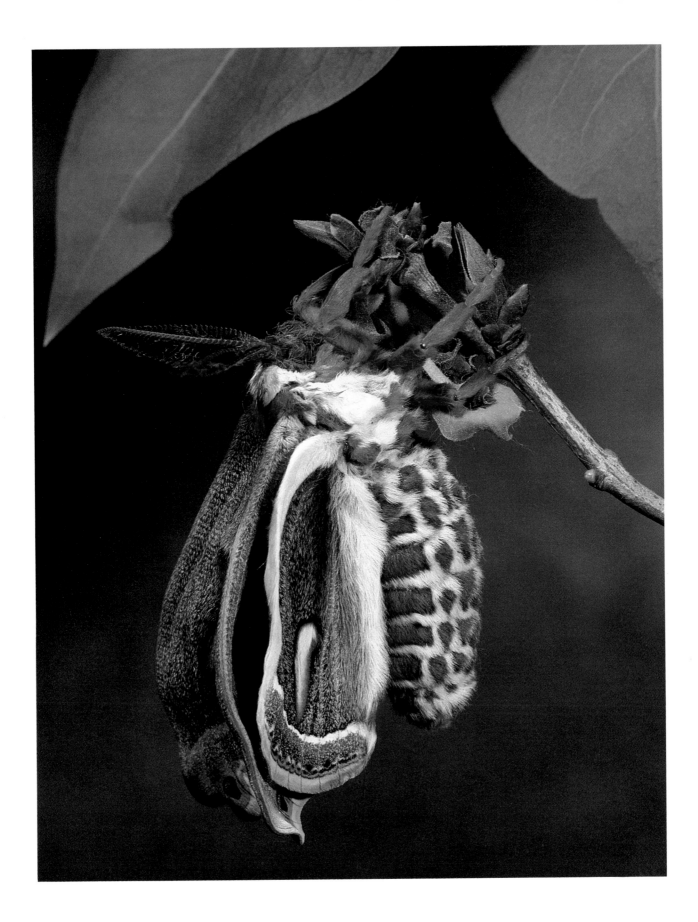

In just a half hour your wings were as big as they are now, but they were still soft and limp. It's taken all afternoon for them to stiffen so you can fly.

My brother blows—very gently—through the screen to help you take off.

And now you're airborne and away. Good-bye, moth! I may never see you again. But I'll look for your caterpillars in summer and their cocoons in the fall. And next spring I may meet another brand-new cecropia moth—and get to know it, too, before it flies away.

MORE ABOUT
CECROPIA MOTHS

Where does the cecropia moth get its name?

The cecropia (sih-KRO-pee-ah) moth is named for King Cecropius, who was (in Greek myths) the first king of Athens.

Where do cecropia moths live?

From southern Canada to northern Florida, Texas, and Mexico. With a wingspread of up to 6 inches (15 centimeters), the cecropia is thought to be the largest moth in North America.

What makes the patterns on the moth's wings and body?

Tiny scales on the moth's wings and body form the patterns of color, the way hairs make different colors in a cat's fur. The scales have short pedicels (stems) that fit into sockets in the moth's wings, which are actually colorless. The scales overlap like shingles. They sometimes brush off as powder if you touch them.

*Do a moth's wings get soggy
when it rains?*

No. The scales on the moth's wings and body have a thin coating of wax. The wax acts like a raincoat and keeps the moth from getting soaked—even if it falls into a puddle.

*How do antennae help the
male moth find the female?*

Each tiny branch of the moth's large feathery antennae is loaded with sense glands. These glands can pick up a female moth's smell from as far away as 4 miles (6 kilometers). Sense glands on other parts of the moth's body play a part, too.

*What does the female moth
use her antennae for?*

Mostly to find food plants on which to deposit her eggs. The female also tests plants with taste organs on the ends of her legs.

Can moths see in the dark?

In spite of its big bulging eyes, the moth can barely tell light from shadows. To fly at night without bumping into things, the moth depends mostly on its keen senses of smell and touch.

Why do moths flutter around lights?

We don't know exactly why. We just know that moths *are* attracted to light, which is why you see them clustered around lightbulbs and windows at night. Many fly into candles and campfires—and die in the flames.

Does a caterpillar have eyes?

Not like a moth's. But it has, on each side of its head, a row of six small, simple eyespots (called ocelli) that help it find the trunks of trees and leafy food.

How do caterpillars eat?

Because a caterpillar's main activity is eating, it has big, powerful mouthparts (mandibles, or jaws), good for chewing plant food—even wood.

How do caterpillars breathe?

Through openings called spiracles along the caterpillar's sides. Each spiracle is connected to an air tube inside the caterpillar's body.

Does a caterpillar have bones?

No. It has a long, wormlike body in thirteen segments (rings) in three sections.

How many legs does a caterpillar have?

Six short legs with claws are on the front section of the caterpillar's body. The caterpillar uses these to hold onto the leaves it eats, but it cannot walk on them. Instead, it crawls on those fat, fleshy stumps you see behind the legs. These are called "prolegs" or "claspers." There are usually five pairs of prolegs. They will disappear when the caterpillar becomes a moth. The prolegs have flat suction-cup soles and little curved hooks that hold tight to surfaces—even your finger. (No, they won't hurt you, just tickle.)

*What are those warty-looking knobs
down the caterpillar's back?*

They are small red and yellow bulbs, or tubercles (sometimes called "little jewels"). They have no use—except maybe to scare off enemies such as birds, snakes, raccoons, and other insect-eaters.

*How does a caterpillar spin
its cocoon?*

Substances from two glands combine to make one silken thread that spins out through its spinneret. The thread hardens when it hits the air. Many cocoons are made of white or yellowish threads. But the cecropia moth spins 4,000 to 5,000 feet (1,200 to 1,500 meters) of dark brown thread—which is why its cocoon is brown.

*What happens to the caterpillar
inside the cocoon?*

When the cocoon is complete, the caterpillar chews a small hole in one end of the cocoon where it will come out in the spring. The caterpillar then becomes a pupa (or chrysalis). Inside the pupa, the caterpillar's body goes through a process called "metamorphosis" as the caterpillar changes from a green wormlike creature into a furry-bodied, big-eyed, splendid-winged moth.

*Why do moths die so soon after
they come out of the cocoon?*

Adult cecropia moths do not eat. For as long as they live, they are nourished by the food they stored up when they were caterpillars. The male usually lives one day, the female two or three days—giving her time to locate a suitable food tree and lay her eggs.

*What keeps the moth's eggs from
falling off the leaves they are laid on?*

The moth cements her tiny eggs with a sticky liquid that comes from a gland in her body. The glue quickly dries, holding the egg bunches (about 12 to an inch) to the leaves until the caterpillars hatch in about 10 days.

*How can I get to know a
cecropia moth?*

It's easy—if you live where cecropias live. One way is to capture a big green caterpillar in the summer. Keep it in a cool, shady place in a clean box or bottle with holes for air and leaves for food. After the caterpillar starts making its cocoon, you can put a light behind the cocoon and watch the caterpillar do its "spinning dance" as it begins to build its cocoon walls. After a while, the walls become too thick to see through.

Or, in fall and winter, you can look for a brown cocoon attached to the bare branch of an apple, willow, lilac, or maple tree. Keep the branch all winter on your porch or in some other cold, outdoor place. (Don't take the cocoon indoors; the moth will hatch too soon—before there are plenty of leaves for its caterpillars to feed on.)

Then, beginning in May, keep a close lookout. The first thing you may notice is the cocoon moving slightly. Listen for a faint rustling sound as the moth struggles to get out, butting her head against the cocoon wall. Watch for a damp stain at the end of the cocoon as the moth softens the casing with liquid. At that spot, you'll soon see the moth emerge. She won't need any help, even if she tumbles to the ground. Just stand close by as her wings expand and she gathers the strength to fly off into the night. Now examine the empty cocoon. Cut it in half. Feel how silky the lining is inside the papery shell.

ABOUT THE AUTHOR AND PHOTOGRAPHER

Freelance editor and author Elizabeth Ring has written extensively for young readers, and natural history topics have often been the focus of her work. A former teacher and an editor at *Ranger Rick,* she has written a range of programs on environmental subjects for the National Wildlife Federation. Her previous books for The Millbrook Press include two biographies, *Rachel Carson: Caring for the Earth* and *Henry David Thoreau: In Step With Nature,* as well as the *Good Dogs!* series. She lives in Woodbury, Connecticut.

Photographer Dwight Kuhn is well known for his studies of nature subjects, especially the beautifully composed close-ups that have appeared often in *Ranger Rick, World, National Geographic, Natural History,* and other magazines. Among his previous books for children are four that were named Outstanding Science Trade Books by the National Science Teachers Association and the Children's Book Council: *The Hidden Life of the Meadow, The Hidden Life of the Pond, The Hidden Life of the Forest,* and *More Than Just a Vegetable Garden.* He lives in Dexter, Maine.